YOUR KNOWLEDGE HAS VALUE

- We will publish your bachelor's and master's thesis, essays and papers

- Your own eBook and book - sold worldwide in all relevant shops

- Earn money with each sale

Upload your text at www.GRIN.com
and publish for free

Bibliographic information published by the German National Library:

The German National Library lists this publication in the National Bibliography; detailed bibliographic data are available on the Internet at http://dnb.dnb.de .

This book is copyright material and must not be copied, reproduced, transferred, distributed, leased, licensed or publicly performed or used in any way except as specifically permitted in writing by the publishers, as allowed under the terms and conditions under which it was purchased or as strictly permitted by applicable copyright law. Any unauthorized distribution or use of this text may be a direct infringement of the author s and publisher s rights and those responsible may be liable in law accordingly.

Imprint:

Copyright © 2018 GRIN Verlag
Print and binding: Books on Demand GmbH, Norderstedt Germany
ISBN: 9783668721296

This book at GRIN:

https://www.grin.com/document/428182

Elena da Silva

The Theme of Madness in "Mrs Dalloway"

GRIN Verlag

GRIN - Your knowledge has value

Since its foundation in 1998, GRIN has specialized in publishing academic texts by students, college teachers and other academics as e-book and printed book. The website www.grin.com is an ideal platform for presenting term papers, final papers, scientific essays, dissertations and specialist books.

Visit us on the internet:

http://www.grin.com/

http://www.facebook.com/grincom

http://www.twitter.com/grin_com

Proseminararbeit

RWTH Aachen University

Institut für Anglistik, Amerikanistik und Romanistik

Lehrstuhl für Anglistische Literaturwissenschaft

The Theme of Madness in Mrs Dalloway

für das Proseminar

What is Modernism?

WS 2017/2018

von Elena da Silva Teixeira

im Rahmen des Bachelorstudienganges Literatur- und Sprachwissenschaft

Mönchengladbach, den 19.03.2018

Table of Contents

1. Introduction 3
2. Madness 4
3. Virginia Woolf's Biography 5
4. Mrs Dalloway 6
   4.1 Clarissa Dalloway 6
   4.2 Septimus Warren Smith 7
   4.3 Dr. Holmes and Sir Williams 9
   4.4 Lucrezia Warren Smith 10
5. Conclusion 11
6. Works Cited 13

1. Introduction

The early 20th century was a troubling time for many. The first World War, which lasted from 1914 to 1918, left behind many wounded people. But it was not just physical scars that the battles have caused. Many British civilians and soldiers had to deal with different types of madness like shell shock, today known as posttraumatic stress disorder, that brought along many other problems such as isolation, repression and social degradation.

The main thesis of this paper is that madness plays a substantial role in the novel which represents Woolf's private life in a lot of ways but also the influence the first world war had on Britain's society and their mental health.

To investigate the representation and role of madness in Virginia Woolf's novel "Mrs Dalloway", this paper will be opened by a brief definition of madness and its different types that were relevant for Britain during the early 20th century, followed by a summary of Virginia Woolf's own biography in order to understand the role madness plays in her novel. Those sections will be compiled by the help of adequate secondary literature.

I will then apply the elaborated aspects to the novel's main character Clarissa Dalloway. Is Clarissa affected by the war and if so, how does it show? Has madness impacted her in any way? The following subsection is concerned with Septimus Warren Smith and his experience with madness and the effect the war had on him. Why does he behave the way he does and how does his madness show? The final subsections will determine how society, especially Dr. Holmes and Sir William Bradshaw, view madness and the way they contemplate and handle mental illnesses in others. I then will give a short outlook on Lucrezia Warren Smith and her relationship to Septimus and the doctors.

At the end, this paper will summarize the most important points as well as answer the opening questions. Furthermore, it will be examined whether there are parallels between the character's and Woolf's private life and what role these play. It will also be discussed whether the thesis was proven right or wrong.

2. Madness

World War I lasted for four years, it began in July of 1914 and ended in November of 1918. Those four years costed numerous victims – physically and mentally.

Post-war anxiety was very prominent among Britain's population in the early 20th century. People suffering from anxiety disorders may experience panic attacks, phobias or discomfort when they are surrounded by people. This might lead to them avoiding certain situations, for example leaving their houses or spending time with their friends and families and pursuing hobbies. They often isolate themselves.

Depression is another important mental illness which many British people suffered from during the time of and after the war. Depression describes the emotional state of being sad or lacking emotion, it can be episodic or permanent. (Kanter 3). People suffering from a depressive disorder experience a row of symptoms, including "loss of interest in activities, sleep and appetite changes, guilt and hopelessness, fatigue, restlessness, concentration problems" (Kanter 4). The disorder often results in death, usually by suicide.

The most prominent consequence of the war amongst soldiers was 'shell shock', which is now known as posttraumatic stress disorder. The term derived from "an attempt to describe cases that arose in the context of exploding ordnance but where enduring symptoms could not be linked to the presence of an obvious organic lesion" (Jones 1641). Shell Shock was originally believed to be linked to physical brain injury, for example by exploding shells. That was until doctors learned that soldiers who did not endure head wounds also experienced symptoms of it (Jones 1642). The most common symptoms are nervousness, amnesia, a pessimistic attitude, social retreat and a personality change (Steil and Rosner 2). There are also physical evidences, such as abdominal ache, cephalea as well as regressive and aggressive behavior. Furthermore, those who are affected often show signs of a fear of the dark or being alone and sleep disturbances (Steil and Rosner 3). They often feel responsible for their own misery and regularly experience flashbacks (Steil and Rosner 4). Shell Shock is strongly linked to Schizophrenia and Paraphrenia, where the diagnosed experience hallucinations and paranoid delusions (Henke 14).

Trauma survivors are often unable to think of their grim experiences in a chronological order and fail to comprehend that they are no longer part of their lives. They believe that they are ever-present and are "unable to integrate the traumatic event into [their] personal [lives]" (DeMeester 200). Since the traumatic experience has destroyed their past beliefs and ideologies, it is important for them to "find new, more reliable ideologies to give order and meaning to [their] post-traumatic [lives]" (DeMeester 199), so that they can recover and overcome it.

3. Virginia Woolf's Biography

Virginia Woolf was born in January of 1882 in London and died in March of 1941 in Sussex. Her father, Leslie Stephen, who was a writer himself, was "unnaturally sensitive, desperate for his mother's approval and sympathy" when he was a child (Welsh 7). Virginia Woolf would adopt those attributions of his. In 1862 he married Harriet Marian who soon gave birth to their first daughter Laura. Laura happened to be mentally disabled. After just eight years of marriage, Harriet passed away (Welsh 8).

He later met Virginia's mother Julia Prinsep Jackson, who took care of her own mother and found comfort in the feeling of being needed and the power it gave to her (Welsh 9). The relationship between Leslie and Julia was not necessarily a healthy one:

> He needed Julia to talk him to sleep and convince him that his was not a wasted life. Julia responded by claiming that it hurt her how much he loved her, that she feared always hurting him because she was not worthy of his love, and she too suffered from over-extending herself. (Welsh 11)

The marriage between her parents influenced Virginia and she entered new relationships with distrust, tense and passive-aggressiveness (Welsh 11). Because their mother took care of her sick relatives, the Woolf children were constantly surrounded by illness and death (Welsh 10). Julia herself died in 1895. Her mother's death led the young woman into depression and Virginia began to feel things more intensively. "All life became overwhelmingly intense, increasing the excitement of an already overwrought young girl" (Welsh 15). Shortly after, her half-sister Stella died from peritonitis and her father abused her sister Vanessa (Welsh 16) before he died in 1904. Virginia herself was abused by her step brothers (Welsh 20).

These events led to her hearing voices and she stopped eating. Desperate and plagued by her declining mental health, she committed her first suicide attempt by jumping out of a window in 1904 (Welsh 18). Many more deaths of family members were to follow, and Virginia's mental health worsened.

She suffered from manic-depressive psychoses and eventually died by suicide in March of 1941 (Welsh 38). This time, she drowned herself. Given she had already failed to commit suicide two times before, she filled the pockets of her coat with stones (Welsh 65). Her death was an act of despair.

4. Mrs Dalloway

In the following paragraphs, I will adapt the elaborated aspects to the characters Clarissa Dalloway, Septimus Warren Smith, Dr. Holmes and Sir Williams Bradshaw from Virginia Woolf's novel "Mrs Dalloway" which takes place in a day in the early 1920s. The goal is to show how madness is displayed and whether it is represented in a realistic manner. I will then give an outlook on Lucrezia Warren Smith to show the perception of madness by someone who is neither a professional, nor a person affected.

4.1 Clarissa Dalloway

Clarissa is a middle-aged woman from London who is preparing a party she is having that evening. She is married to Richard Dalloway, by whom she has a daughter named Elizabeth. Her marriage allows her to live a life of glamour, but both of them, Clarissa and Richard, have difficulties expressing their feelings for each other. Richard buys Clarissa flowers, but he cannot get himself to tell her that he loves her (Woolf 129). Mrs. Dalloway's real love, however, is Peter Walsh, with whom she used to share a close relationship in her youth. When meeting him again after several years, her feelings for him arise: "She looked at Peter Walsh; her look, passing through all that time and that emotion . . ." (Woolf 47). This meeting makes Clarissa question her life choices. She wonders what would have been different if she did not marry Richard but Peter instead, which is a theme that can be found throughout her entire life.

It is hard for Clarissa to communicate her emotions; thus, she mostly has to handle them herself. Loneliness and Isolation take control over her existence. Introspection plays a substantial role in her life. Even Peter, who is still in love with her, tells her that she has a cold nature: "Clarissa came up, with her perfect manners, like a real hostess, and wanted to introduce him to some one – spoke as if they had never met before, which enraged him" (Woolf 67). This makes Clarissa "wince" (Woolf 67), which indicates that she has not really noticed that trait of hers before.

Even when doing trivial activities, Clarissa Dalloway can feel her overthinking and anxiety overcome her. This has also been the case before she had to experience the war:

> How fresh, how calm, stiller than this of course, the air was in the early morning; . . . chill and sharp and yet (for a girl of eighteen as she then was) solemn, feeling as she did, standing there at the open window, that something awful was about to happen…(Woolf 3)

Those bad thoughts seem to come out of nowhere, for no particular reason. Possible triggers are a repressed trauma from her sister's death, whom Clarissa witnessed being killed by a falling tree (Woolf 85), and later, her regret of marrying Richard Dalloway over Peter Walsh. Her lack of ability to communicate her emotions is intensifying her mental health issues. Being the wife on a successful upper-class man also evokes the pressure in her to be a presentable woman. Although she enjoys having parties at her home, it is also means a lot of pressure for her because she is anxious something going wrong. Furthermore, she does not like the feeling of someone being superior to her (Woolf 12).

At her party, Mrs. Dalloway learns about Septimus' death. Instead of feeling bad for him and his desperate act, she feels a connection for him that displays Clarissa's attitude towards life: "She felt somehow very like him – the young man who had killed himself. She felt glad that he had done it; thrown it away while they went on living" (Woolf 204).

4.2 Septimus Warren Smith

Septimus Warren Smith used to be a young smart man who was interested in literature. He is married to an Italian woman called Rezia who takes care of him. Rezia has always admired Septimus for his literacy (Woolf 98).

The reason Septimus wanted to be a soldier was to become a man and show his commitment to Britain (Woolf 94). When he returned from fighting as a soldier in World War I, he underwent a personality change. In the battles, he witnessed his officer Evans, who also was a friend of his, die. First, Smith deliberately ignores his sadness; ". . . when Evans was killed, . . . Septimus, far from showing any emotion or recognising that here was the end of a friendship, congratulated himself upon feeling very little and very reasonably" (Woolf 94, 95). Ultimately, this would lead – along with other factors – to a posttraumatic stress disorder.

Warren Smith has neither processed his friend's death, nor the experiences he has made in the battles himself. He is not a smart, literate man anymore, but a shell-shocked war veteran. His experiences during the war led to him being numb and not feeling anything on the one hand (Woolf 95), but also being delusional on the other. The reason he married Rezia was to prove to himself that he is indeed able to feel something, but it failed (Woolf 95). He regularly hallucinates and often sees Evans, for example when he was at home waiting for his wife: "It was at that moment (Rezia had gone shopping) that the great revelation took place. A voice spoke from behind the screen. Evans was speaking. The dead were with him" (Woolf 102). Clearly, he has not come to terms with his and Evan's destiny yet.

Septimus happens to feel guilty for the acts he had done during war. When he is sitting in the park he beings to hallucinate and hears birds singing "words how there is no crime and, joined by another sparrow, they sang in voices prolonged and piercing in Greek words, from trees in the meadow of life beyond a river where the dead walk, how there is no death" (Woolf 26). This indicates that Septimus has killed one or multiple people during the battle and is trying to repress those memories.

Septimus is treated by Dr. Holmes and Sir William Bradshaw, but they do not take his complaints serious and instead order him inadequate treatments (Woolf 99, 108). They only worsen his demise. Sir Williams wants Septimus to go to an asylum for the lunatic which ultimately leads him into committing suicide. The moment Septimus fears Dr. Holmes is coming to get him into the asylum is one of the few moments he is actually thinking clear:

> Holmes was coming upstairs. Holmes would burst open the door . . . The gas fire? But it was too late now. Holmes was coming. Razors he might have got, but Rezia, who always did that sort of thing, had packed them. There remained only the window, the large Bloomsbury lodging-house window; the tiresome, the troublesome, and rather melodramatic business of opening the window and throwing himself out. (Woolf 163)

He is able to think precisely and linear and experiences reasonable fear. This suggests that his anticipation for death allows him to be himself again. Knowing that his misery will soon come to an end leads to him becoming mentally stable again – since his madness results from the inability to integrate his trauma into his personal life.

4.3 Dr. Holmes and Sir Williams

Holmes is a doctor who takes care of Septimus Warren Smith. However, he does not take the trauma caused by the war serious. He does not believe that there is something seriously wrong with Septimus: "There was nothing whatever the matter . . ." (Woolf 99). Instead, he orders him to distract himself by doing activities that bring other people joy, including Dr. Holmes himself (Woolf 99), such as playing golf and going to the music hall (Woolf 99). When Septimus commits suicide, Dr. Holmes does not feel pitiful or question his methods but instead calls him a "coward" for giving up on life (Woolf 164). Although he has been treating Septimus who had often announced his suicide attempt, he did not see his self-imposed death coming and thinks it was imprudent: "A sudden impulse, no one was in the least to blame . . . And why the devil he did it, Dr. Holmes could not conceive" (Woolf 164).

Sir William Bradshaw is a psychiatrist who also treats Septimus Warren Smith. Clarissa Dalloway went to see several times, too. He is well respected by society because "He had worked very hard; he had won his position by sheer ability (being the son of a shopkeeper); loved his profession; made a fine figurehead at ceremonies and spoke well . . ." (Woolf 104). However, he is not very empathetic and believes in science rather than feelings. He is a strong believer of proportion and wants his patients to share his beliefs and act according to their position:

> Worshipping proportion, Sir William not only prospered himself but made England prosper, secluded her lunatics, forbade childbirth, penalised despair, made it impossible for the unfit to propagate their views until they, too, shared his sense of proportion . . . (Woolf 109)

Furthermore, he presumes his colleague's respect for his work, he wants his "subordinates" to fear him and his patients' gratitude (Woolf 109). He is highly confident in his abilities. Another evidence for Sir William preferring rational over emotional thinking and acting is his adoration of conversion. "But Proportion has a sister . . . Conversion is her name and she feasts on the wills of the weakly, loving to impress, to impose, adoring her own features stamped on the face of the populace" (Woolf 109). In contrast to Dr. Holmes, he notices that there is something wrong with Septimus:

> He could see the first moment they came into the room (the Warren Smiths they were called); he was certain directly he saw the man; it was a case of extreme gravity. It was a case of extreme breakdown – complete physical and nervous breakdown, with every symptom in an advanced stage, he ascertained in two or three minutes . . .(Woolf 104, 105)

However, he does not take his threat to commit suicide serious and says that "we all have our moments of depression" (Woolf 107). He does not think that Septimus is mad but rather that he does not have "a sense of proportion" (Woolf 106).

To treat Septimus' lunacy he chooses methods that can be considered highly marginal by today's standard of knowledge. He requests that when a patient is ill and threatens to kill himself, "you invoke proportion; order rest in bed; rest in solitude; silence and rest; rest without friends, without books, without messages; six months rest; until a man who went in weighing seven stone six comes out weighing twelve" (Woolf 108). Sir William is confident in his treatment. Bradshaw wanting to put him into an asylum for the mentally unstable ultimately leads to Septimus' suicide (Woolf 163, 164).

Both doctors think people who had gone mad should be locked away, so Britain's population does not have to witness the trauma the war has caused (Woolf 109).

4.4 Lucrezia Warren Smith

Lucrezia Warren Smith is Septimus' wife. She is a young hat maker from Italy, but she moved to London with her husband. She met Septimus in Italy (Woolf 94, 95). Back then, Septimus was a healthy man who enjoyed reading Shakespeare. Rezia was in love with him and admired him. She even wanted to have a son like him, although she feared "nobody could be like Septimus; so gentle; so serious; so clever" (Woolf 98).

After the war, her perception of her husband changes. He has become a lunatic and although Rezia still loves him, she often is ashamed. She is scared other people will think badly of her and her husband when they are out in public. When her husband threatens to kill himself in town, she first thinks of the other people's opinion of them: "People must notice; people must see. People, she thought, looking at the crowd staring at the motor car . . . Suppose they had heard him? . . . But failure once conceals. She must take him into some park" (Woolf 16, 17).

Lucrezia wants Septimus to be healthy again. Therefore, she tolerates the doctors' treatments. She dislikes Sir William because he has deserted her. What is worse for her, however, is that he wants to tear her and her husband apart (Woolf 108).

The first time she understands Septimus is when he commits suicide. She does not get angry at him for leaving her alone, but instead respects his decision: "'He is dead', she said, smiling at the poor old woman . . ." (Woolf 165).

5. Conclusion

"Mrs Dalloway" is a novel in which we learn about the lives of many different Londoners. Although not all of them meet each other and some of them do not even know about each other's existence, there is a connection between them. They all have to master their lives in post-war London. Some of them are able to live their lives as before, while others suffer from the consequences of World War I.

Madness as a consequence of the belligerent times is the main theme of the novel. The doctors function as prime examples for people who do not take the suffering many soldiers and civilians had to endure seriously. They are proud to be British and wish for those affected to suffer in silence, so they can continue to live peacefully and undisturbed. They represent a part of Britain's society which has not accepted the trauma that was caused. Rezia on the other hand represents those who do feel compassion for those affected. She feels pitiful for her husband and wants him to become healthy again. When he commits suicide, Rezia can comprehend and respects his decision to do so because she can in fact understand why someone would not want to live a life as his. She accepts the trauma induced by the war. However, she also fears what other people might think about her husband and is therefore well aware of the fact that there are people who do not sympathize with war veterans – like Holmes and Bradshaw.

Clarissa Dalloway and Septimus Warren Smith represent those who were driven insane by the time they lived in. Clarissa shows typical signs of an anxiety disorder – she does not have many friends or any particular hobbies. It is hard for her to express her feelings or show excitement. Furthermore, she appears to be getting sad out of nowhere. She does throw parties regularly, however, she usually spends them sitting in her room alone watching her neighbors from afar. She is constantly anxious about making a mistake or being overtrumped by someone. Clarissa Dalloway shows realistic signs of an anxiety disorder. Septimus Warren Smith shows a row of symptoms pointing towards depression. He is hopeless, feels guilty and is tired of life. He turned from a well-read Shakespeare lover to a lunatic man. Septimus underwent a personality change which is typical for people suffering from a posttraumatic stress disorder. Additionally, he also experiences flashbacks and even hallucinates, mostly about his comrade Evans. The young man is not able to comprehend that this period of his life is over and cannot integrate it into his current life. He is unable to recover from the trauma and therefore decides to commit suicide. Septimus is also a good way of illustrating Posttraumatic stress disorder, schizophrenia and depression.

There are several similarities between the character's and Virginia Woolf's lives. Similarly to Rezia, she too had a family member who was not considered "normal" by society at that time since her sister Laura was mentally handicapped. Just like Clarissa Dalloway, Virginia Woolf had difficulties expressing her feelings. Also, both of them are are constantly looking for approval and sympathy. However, Woolf shares the biggest parallels with Septimus. Virginia and Septimus both suffer from a manic depression. Both of their illnesses were caused by depressed traumata. Virginia became depressed after her sister and her mother died, Septimus' madness was also triggered by the death of a loved person, at least partly. The two of them have not processed their traumatic experiences. Septimus' suicide is another parallel to Virginia Woolf's life. Woolf attempted suicide by jumping out of a window, which is how Septimus dies. Woolf uses these characters to represent her own life, but also to process her experiences. She has witnessed two world wars and wants to show the effect wars have on people's mental health and their lives.

6. Works Cited

DeMeester, Karen. *Trauma and Recovery in Virginia Woolf's "Mrs. Dalloway"*. Baltimore: The Johns Hopkins University Press, 2009. Online.

Henke, Suzette. *Virginia Woolf's Septimus Smith*. New York: State University of New York. 1981. Online.

Jones, Edgar et al. *Shell Shock and Mild Traumatic Brain Injury: A Historical Review*. The American Journal of Psychiatry, Vol. 164, No. 11. 2007. Online.
https://doi.org/10.1176/appi.ajp.2007.07071180

Kanter, Jonathan W. et al. *The Nature of Clinical Depression: Symptoms, Syndromes, and Behavior Analysis*. The Behavior Analyst, Vol. 31, No. 1. 2008. Online.
https://link.springer.com/article/10.1007/BF03392158

Leese, Peter. *Shell Shock: Traumatic Neurosis and the British Soldiers of the first World War*. Berlin Heidelberg: Springer Verlag. 2002. Online.
Steil, Regina, and Rita Rosner. *Posttraumatische Belastungsstörung*. Göttingen: Hogrefe Verlag. 2008. Print.

Welsh, Camille-Yvette. *Biography of Virginia Woolf*. Philadelphia: Chelsea House Publishers. 2005. Online.

Woolf, Virgina. *Mrs Dalloway*. London: Penguin Classics. 2000. Print.

YOUR KNOWLEDGE HAS VALUE

- We will publish your bachelor's and master's thesis, essays and papers

- Your own eBook and book - sold worldwide in all relevant shops

- Earn money with each sale

Upload your text at www.GRIN.com
and publish for free